Remembrance and Gratitude

Book 3

A Selection of Poems and Writings

by

Charles F. Meek

CCB Publishing
Terrace, British Columbia, Canada

Remembrance and Gratitude Book 3:
A Selection of Poems and Writings

Copyright ©2017 by Charles F. Meek
ISBN-13   978-1-77143-329-7
First Edition

Library and Archives Canada Cataloguing in Publication
Meek, Charles F., 1943-, author
Remembrance and gratitude book 3 : a selection of poems and writings /
by Charles F. Meek. -- First edition.
Issued in print and electronic formats.
ISBN 978-1-77143-329-7 (pbk.).--ISBN 978-1-77143-330-3 (pdf)
Cataloguing data available from Library and Archives Canada

All poems and essays contained herein are copyright Charles F. Meek.

Photos contained herein are either copyright Charles F. Meek or provided courtesy of the copyright owner.

Extreme care has been taken by the author to ensure that all information presented in this book is accurate and up to date at the time of publishing. Neither the author nor the publisher can be held responsible for any errors or omissions. Additionally, neither is any liability assumed for damages resulting from the use of the information contained herein.

All rights reserved. No part of this publication may be reproduced, stored in a retrieval system or transmitted in any form or by any means, electronic, mechanical, photocopying, recording or otherwise without the express written permission of the publisher, except by a reviewer who may quote brief passages in a review to be printed in a newspaper, magazine, or journal.

Publisher: CCB Publishing
             Terrace, British Columbia, Canada
             www.ccbpublishing.com

This book is dedicated to you, the reader.

Thank you all far and wide.

Yours in Friendship,
Charlie

Foreword

In today's fast-paced and sometimes turbulent world it is refreshing to take a moment to pause and reflect upon the many blessings we have in our lives. Charles F. Meek's writings allow you to do just that.

He reminds us all of the sacrifices made by Veterans who have gone off to war years ago, and also in more recent times, recalling that the price of freedom is never free. Those soldiers who are lucky enough to return home also struggle with the effects of war for the rest of their lives, often in silence.

Our ancestors and origins are important to our sense of self and place in this world. Charlie demonstrates through the written word that he is grateful for the sacrifices made by his parents, grandparents and others so that he has been able to go on to make a better life for himself and his family.

His sense of community, charity and friendship is honourable, and encourages us all to lend a helping hand when we can. It is only by helping one another that we can make this a better world for ourselves, our children and generations still to come.

Charlie's love and devotion to his wife Eleanor is heartwarming. Together they have had a long, loving marriage, constantly showing unending support and encouragement for each other.

I am grateful for Charlie's kindness and friendship, and also to have been able to assist him in bringing his work to readers near and far.

Paul Rabinovitch
Publisher
CCB Publishing

Praise for *Remembrance and Gratitude*

I knew Charlie Meek long before he knew me. Let me explain.

I love radio. Ever since I was 5 or 6 I listened to whatever station I could find up and down the dial from all over the province, the country and the states.

It was the personalities I enjoyed the most, it didn't matter the music. (I'm a classic rock guy mostly.)

As I got older growing up in Terrace and Prince Rupert, B.C. radio grew up with me adding a station to the two already here. As a teenager I was still listening to the personalities.

I found A Touch O' Whiteheather on the new radio station CJFW in Terrace. I found the host very committed to the music, the home he was from and the place he now lived.

By the time I moved back to Terrace when I was 18, I found myself working at the same station where he worked.

Charlie was in and out and said Hi to this young teenager, wished me the best with a big smile, and offered to help me with anything I needed.

Flash forward ten years and Terrace grows up some more with another radio station, CFNR, where I now work.

I find myself chatting about Remembrance Day and First Nations Veterans and help Charlie get Remembrance Day services on the radio.

Since then I have had and still do have a friendship with Charlie, and have had the honour of hosting on TV and the Internet Remembrance Day services with him.

His commitment to Veterans, seniors and to Terrace is amazing. He is always on the go, and where he finds the energy I don't know… he is the busiest guy I know.

Thank you, Charlie, for your friendship, your insight on our community and continued commitment to Veterans and seniors.

I ask everyone to enjoy the poems in this book as we get to know our wonderful amazing part of the world, including the people in it and my friend Charlie Meek, just a little more.

Steve Little

Preface

Here is the final book in the trilogy of *Remembrance and Gratitude*.

Over the past few years I have been blessed in being able to write the poems in these books, many of the works are dedications to friends and people I know and have known, from far and wide.

There are so many people I would like to thank, first and foremost my wife Eleanor for encouraging me to put my words into book form.

My friends Bill and Norma Young of Terrace, B.C. who started me off in writing, also Bill and Helene McRae for their ongoing support.

To Paul and Donna from CCB Publishing in Terrace, B.C., their work in assisting me and ensuring an excellent publication of my book, a big thank you to you both.

My tributes to the R.C.M.P., to my Thornhill Fire Department, the Royal Canadian Legion, Branch 13, Terrace, B.C. and the Mills Memorial Hospital staff and doctors.

To all our Veterans. And to many personal friends. I thank you all.

I recall my very first poem that I wrote; I was at the bedside of a dear lady, Vesta Douglas of Terrace. My living tribute to her, I am happy to say when the Scottish Fiddle Orchestra came to our hometown, we had Mrs. Douglas in the audience and unknown to her, and along with music from the orchestra I read the poem to her. Many in the audience had tears in their eyes. She was a lovely lady and I am glad that I knew her.

And to you the reader, I thank you sincerely for purchasing the books and I hope you have enjoyed them as much as I have enjoyed writing them. Thank you.

Yours in friendship,
Charlie

Contents

Foreword v
Praise for *Remembrance and Gratitude* vii
Preface ix
What My Dad Did 1
Volunteers Dedication 2
Unknown But to God 3
Time Goes By 4
The Old Warrior 5
The Old Picture Frame 6
The Golden Fall 7
Remembering Our Heroes 8
Our Opa 9
Our Angel on the Tree 10
My Legends 11
My Hometown, Terrace, B.C. 12
My Heroes of Old 13
My Friends 14
Memories in Time 15
Mayerthorpe Remembered 16
Lay Me Down 17
The Days of Old 18
His Fight for Freedom 19
Heroes Never Die 20

Forever Young 21
Dedication for Constable Sarah Beckett 22
Days of Old 23
Friendship 24
My Dear Old Grannie 25
A Soldier's Valour 26
A Soldier He Was 27
A Piper of Renown, Keith Easdale 28
A Grandson's Question 29
A Christmas Blessing 30
A Baby Is Born 31
Some Additional Poems 32
About the Author 33

What My Dad Did

When I was but a child you taught me right from wrong
You taught me the words of your favourite song
You raised me up to respect my elders and peers
If I stepped out of line, well a slap across the ears.

You were my dad, a coal miner you were
You came home at night and you were always there
Time went by and I grew up to be a man
You taught me well for now I am who I am.

I help others whenever the need does arise
I see the thank you, I see it in their eyes
No thanks is needed for the things I do
For you raised me up, for that I thank you.

Then the day came when you left me here alone
In Heaven's pathways I pray you can roam
I am a better person for what you taught all those many years ago
It saddens me to think, when I had to let you go.

You will always be with me each night and every day
For you raised me to speak out and have my say
You were my dad and one day we will meet again
And together we will walk, a place where there is no rain.

You are my dad.

Volunteers Dedication

They are a group of volunteers who dedicate their time
They ensure our safety, our lives often entwine
Thornhill Fire Hall is the place they call home
They are from all walks of life, always close to a phone.

When you see their truck rushing at great speed
Please give way for an emergency someone is in need
Yes they are a group of volunteers who have dedicated their time
They are our friends, yes friends of yours and mine.

Christmas time they decorate the trucks all nice and bright
Drive around our communities trucks with Christmas lights
Wishing us all Christmas greetings and all to be safe
Watch out for them, please give a friendly wave.

They are our men and women from my Thornhill Hall
They are my friends they always give their all
They ask you to drive safe also be safe in your home
Always be safe wherever you may roam.

Dedicated to the memory of
Fireman Dave Beatty

Charles F. Meek

Unknown But to God

I stand here at your resting place
I salute you in remembrance even tho' I don't know your name
They call you the Unknown Soldier, I do not see your face
You fought in foreign battles, our freedom you fought to gain.

No name is carved on the granite stone
All we know is they brought you here, here to your home
And laid you to rest for all of us to see
You were a son, a father, a brother even to me.

No one knows your name, but there is one who does know
He looks down from above, from his Golden Throne
Shines a light upon you, to guide you here to your home
We lay the blood red poppy upon your last resting place
We thank you for your sacrifice the light shines upon your face.

"Lest We Forget"

Time Goes By

The years are going by so fast, oh where has time gone
I look at old-time photos at times I feel so forlorn
I recall being a boy with a song in my heart
Singing for my mother, sadly we are now apart.

Yes the years have gone by quickly and now in my twilight years
Far away from home I shed a silent tear
One day I hope to return even for a short stay
Hopefully to meet you all even for just a day.

Share some laughter and memories of long ago
My heart is still with you, this I want you to know
I am happy to be here in my Canadian life
Making new friends, and here with my loving wife.

The lion still roars inside me for the land where I was a child
One day I will return happiness in my heart will be filled
Each day is a blessing when I see the break of dawn
All the worries in life, all the worries gone
Every day is a blessing, for that I give thanks.

Charles F. Meek

The Old Warrior

He was an old warrior getting close to ninety-eight
He knew he was close, close to Heaven's Gate
He called me on the phone and said he wanted to talk
Well, I went to see him, we went for a nice walk.

He said to me, "My friend my life is almost at an end
I would like to leave, but first make amends
You see I fought in a war where many lives were lost
Often I see them, they are my ghosts
I will leave this world, I hope a better place
I fought to get freedom, victory upon my face
I don't ask for honours, or medals of any kind
I ask remember those who have gone,
remember them for Auld Lang Syne
Put me in that place, where all veterans lie
Where I will be at peace, don't shed a tear or even cry
I have done my life's duty, now I lay me down to lie
Pray for me, I am glad we met
I ask you to pray and Lest We Forget."

The Old Picture Frame

Who do you see in that old picture frame?
An old black and white you do recall the name
Maybe a friend or some family member
Never forget and always remember.

A picture does say many things
Seeing it there a smile to you it brings
That old picture in the old frame hangs on my wall
I remember you well you always gave your all.

You were my dad I did love you dearly
The way I speak this can be seen clearly
I always remember you were always there for me
The day you left I was left to grieve.

That picture in that old picture frame
I proudly look as it bares your name.

Charles F. Meek

The Golden Fall

I love to drive on Sixteen West
Where the scenery is some of the best
In the fall the leaves are golden brown
As I drive from town to town.

Often I will see a bear on the roadside eating
I'll take a picture, that's my kind of greeting
Often a moose will get in your way
Another picture to make my day.

I travel from Terrace to Prince Rupert I am bound
The best of scenery the best all around
Welcome to our Beautiful B.C.
Stay at Kleanza the best park you will see.

Meet old friends coffee by the campfire
Rest and relax that is our desire
Welcome to our Beautiful B.C.
Please leave it as you found it is all free.

Remembering Our Heroes

November the eleventh is close at hand
When I wear my poppy and take my stand
Since last we met some of our Vets have passed
Their memories in our hearts will forever last
Wear your poppy and wear it with pride
Remember our Heroes to them we abide.

Some would have us not wear our poppy red
We wear it for those, those who fought and bled
They fought the enemy so we could be free
They gave their lives for the likes of you and me.

On this Remembrance Day, bow your head and pray
Give thanks to absent friends wear your poppy on this day
Their names engraved in granite, their names firmly set
Please remember them, and Lest We Forget.

Charles F. Meek

Our Opa

Sometimes we lose a loved one who is close and very dear
Do not grieve for long, for they are close and quite near
I know of friends of mine who miss their loved one
They speak of him often, a granddaughter and a grandson.

They miss their dear Opa, they miss him every day
They talk fondly of Opa his memory is here to stay
They will think of you this Christmas at this special time
An empty chair at the table our thoughts entwined.

You will look down upon us a smile from Heaven above
A star on the Christmas tree shining down your love
We know you will be looking down and keeping us all safe
We have your picture in a picture frame,
we look and see your shining face
You are at peace, and so full of grace
We love you Opa.

Dedicated to Opa
From Nicki and Rick

Our Angel on the Tree

When you lose someone, someone loving and dear
Do not mourn, for that loving someone is close and near
They look down upon you, an Angel from the skies
Brushing away the tears, the tears in your eyes.

A Guardian Angel from above, to watch over you
To guide you on your way, the road straight and true
They loved you the way as partners in time you were
Now they have gone, remember they were always there.

A birthday, an anniversary those days they will pass
We will always have you with us, every Christmas
So look down upon us, our Angel in Heaven above
Guide our steps and show us your true love
Be with us this Christmas be the Angel on our tree
Remember long ago, as a child I sat on your knee.

Charles F. Meek

My Legends

I think of all the people, that I knew way back when
Many I recall, many, proudly I knew of them
They were from my hometown where I grew up as a boy
Playing with my pals that was our joy.

There were the Pratts and the Barrs with the Gibsons too
The Lawlors and the Airnes, and of course me and you
There was always a welcome, always an open door
Sadly many have gone, gone on before.

We remember them on special days of the year
Yes we sit and reminisce, and shed a loving tear
Looking down on Lochies Road and the old Duke Street
Where as a boy, I learned to walk on my feet.

Those days of so long ago when life was full of fun
Geordie Gray's buses where we played in the daylight sun
Oh how I wish I could go back to those memorable days
And see all our friends before God took them away.

Today they are legends of my Clackmannan Town
I remember sitting on the dyke in Kerse Green Road
My dad and his friends sat there to lighten their load
Yes they are my Clackmannan Legends and proud I am of them
One day we all hope to meet, and be with them again.

So raise your glass and your elbow you can bend
As we drink a toast, a toast to absent friends.

My Hometown, Terrace, B.C.

I live in a town in the Pacific Northwest
A town called Terrace I consider the best
Where I have many friends of whom I like to greet
We go for a coffee and we are happy to meet.

There is much to see in my hometown
The forest and rivers to the sea they flow on down
The mountains they stand, they stand so tall
The trees in their golden bloom they sparkle in the fall
Yes Terrace is my hometown where I rest my weary head
I give thanks to my friends each night when I go to bed.

From here you can travel by land, sea and air
Have a wonderful time at the Skeena Valley Fall Fair
You can fish for the salmon as they come up to spawn
See all the fishermen on the Skeena at dawn
Yes I love my hometown of Terrace this you will know
Keeping busy, meeting friends, and always on the go.

Thanks to my friend
Bill McCrae for the inspiration.

Charles F. Meek

My Heroes of Old

We all have our heroes, some new and some old
Mine are of olden days, when they stood bold
The days of William Wallace when he stood on Stirling Bridge
And chased the English enemy over the grassy ridge
He set the stage for Bruce aye it was his turn
When he gained Scotland's freedom at a place called Bannockburn.

Then Bonnie Prince Charlie they cried when he waved goodbye
Dressed in paupers' clothes as he left for the Isle of Skye
Then Rob Roy MacGregor he liked to help the poor
A meal on their tables this Rob Roy made sure
Then Walter Scott and Rabbie Burns too
They wrote down their words just for me and you.

Then my most important hero, none more than my old dad
A coal miner he was, I was his youngest lad
He brought us up to be polite, honest and true
A son of Scotland, a friend to all of you
You are my heroes, my heroes of new.

My Friends

I have many friends, First Nations folks around from where I live
From Greenville to Aiyansh and Canyon City my friendship I give
Kitselas to Kitsumkalum and Kitwancool as well
All kinds of friends this I can tell.

There is a young man, who I have known since he was a boy
Now he has grown up and no longer plays with toys
John Wilson is his name, carvings from wood is his fame
He is an artist and a good one I say
Some of his carvings may come your way.

We are proud to know him, we watched him grow tall
He does his work, and he gives his all
I am proud to call many, many of you my friends
I pray our friendship will last until the end.

Charles F. Meek

Memories in Time

It's that time of year again when we think of what has passed
The memories of a loved one, those memories will forever last
New friends who we have met forever at our side
A friendship forever, we pray that will abide.

Old friends we greet and shake a welcome hand
In times of trouble at their side we stand
We see the seasons come, and we see them go
My favourite is the springtime when the flowers are in bloom
Sitting around the campfire, singing a merry tune.

Let us think of the good times, when we all had fun
Watching the children playing games at catch and run
Those were the days when our memories begun
Playing in the fields and basking in the sun.

The years have gone by, now in my twilight years
All the sad memories have gone, along with my hidden fears
Now I sit quietly at home with my loving wife
Reminiscing and thankful that she is my life.

Mayerthorpe Remembered

It has been twelve years since that day from hell
When four police officers doing their duty sadly fell
They were young Constables who gave their all
Constables Gordon, Johnston, Schiemann and Myrol.

A killer shot them on that cold March day
They were doing their duty they are with their God, this I pray
Mayerthorpe made the news Canada wide
Tears fell as all Canadians stood side by side.

Let us not forget these four young men
Let us call their names, again and again
Anthony, Leo, Peter and Brock
They stood together, together like solid rock.

We will remember them each and every year
I will think of them, and shed a silent tear
"We Will Never Forget. We Will Remember Them."
Mayerthorpe Will Be Remembered.

Charles F. Meek

Lay Me Down

He passed away all alone in his home
He wanted a quiet funeral with nobody to grieve his leaving
Just the funeral people to lay him to rest
And no one to do any grieving.

He was an old warrior he fought in a war long gone
He never spoke of that time, he just wanted to forget
No friends or comrades came to visit, he preferred to be alone
He liked to read books, but never had a phone.

No flags to be lowered to half-mast
No prayers are requested just the hymn "Abide With Me"
I go to my maker, and I will be free at last
Lay me down six feet below to rest my weary head
A piece in the paper to let them know I am dead
No flags at half-mast place a poppy on my grave
This is all I ask for the service that I gave
Lay me down six feet below so I can rest my weary head.

The Days of Old

I remember as a young un playin in the street
Runnin up and doon wi gutties on ma feet
Riding ma old bike, nae tires on the wheels
Nae brakes or a seat but it was aw'e the freels.

Then Tam Kettles caught me and took ma bike awa
Noo git on hame, or I'll be tellin yer maw
O'ch these wir the days when we made or ain fun
Chapping at Mrs. Pratt's door and doon the road we wid run.

Stealin Crouther Gordon's apples with a full juke
Ate aw'e the apples at the garage's we puked
A'ch they were fun days, on a Saturday we stayed oot late
Ma big brothers and sisters were oot on a date.

O'ch these wir the fun days in the days of old
Playin wi oor pals, this you will be told
Now I am old, and graceful I often have a laugh
These are my memories of the old days that I have.

Charles F. Meek

His Fight for Freedom

He fought in war for Freedom he fought to bring the enemy down
He was just a young lad, a local lad from our town
Marching with his buddies to do the best they can
They went to foreign lands, a place called Afghanistan.

When his time was over he returned to his homeland
His friends all gathered he shook a welcome hand
Even though he was home, he could not forget the past
The friends that he made, would forever last.

He was just a young boy when he went to war
He came home a man when he walked in the front door
Let us not forget the sacrifice he made in leaving his family behind
Remembering his friends the ones he lost,
remember for Auld Lang Syne.

Pay tribute to this young man and others who went to fight
We will remember you, we will at the coming of the twilight
Each November the eleventh with my hand on my heart
A blood red poppy in my lapel for we aren't too far apart.
"Lest We Forget"

Heroes Never Die

We watched as you sailed away to fight in foreign lands
Standing on the beach bare feet in pristine sands
Children all around waving as the ship sails away
Please come home safely this we do pray.

"Heroes Never Die"

You fought with your comrades fighting for your life
Children here at home also your loving wife
We wait for the day for you to come home
I listen to hear your voice even on the phone.

"Heroes Never Die"

Then the news came that the war was over
In your Bible I placed the four leaf clover
We prayed for your return to come home safe
To see that big smile on your loving face.

"Heroes Never Die"

The good Lord said today you are not mine
Go to your family enjoy the graceful time.

"Heroes Never Die"

Charles F. Meek

Forever Young

I've written about these two people, I've written of them before
They are dear friends of mine, I'm always welcome at their door
Norma and Bill well known in this Terrace town
Always a smile, a hand to shake, and never a frown.

Recently their hearts were broken their spirits pretty low
We were all there for you, this I want you to know
Your beloved Cheryl left this world her pain is no more
Her beloved Adrian missed her so much,
he joined her at Heaven's door.

Bill and Norma are special people in my life I visit when I can
Norma is a special lady, Bill a very kind gentle man
If you see these friends of mine stop and say hello
Shake their hand, they are my friends this I want you to know.

Dedication for Constable Sarah Beckett

She did her duty day in and day out, and this she did well
Working with others was her enjoyment this you could tell
Whenever a child was in danger Sarah would be close at hand
You did your duty you took your stand.

Today I watched as they carried you shoulder high
A flag draped coffin for your journey to Heaven up high
Your comrades solemnly marched row upon row
To honour your memory this we all know.

You leave behind a loving husband and two little boys
As they grow up they will miss their mother's joys
The pipes they played they played just for you
You were a sweetheart to those that you knew.

Your name will be inscribed forever in stone
We will remember you even tho' you have gone
Your duty has now come to an end
Broken hearts will now have to mend
The pipes they played and yes just for you
Rest in Peace Sarah, Rest in Peace.

Charles F. Meek

Days of Old

Dae ye remember playing as bairns playin hide'n'seek
Runnin abbot like crazy and sand shoes on yer feet
Goin up the to-oer fer a Jackdaw fer a pet
Climbin up the chimney fer a stipid bet.

Goin tae Grasso's fer a bag O' chips
Lots O' vinegar an eatin awe the wee bits
Stealin the Meenster's aiples just havin fun
There's old Tom Kettles and then we wid awe run.

Aye those wir the days when nae doors wir locked
Ye wid jist walk in and say hi to old Jock
Ye wid be oot playin late intae the night
Yer maw wid shout on ye come in it's near midnight.

O'h fer those day away back yon
Me and ma big brother, big brother John
A'h hiv the memories of those fun times
Those memories of old they are all mine.

Friendship

Another year over a new one has begun
Let's hope it is full of laughter and lots of fun
Meet up with old friends and make some new
Travel to faraway places with me and just you.

Let us not forget those friends and loved ones who have left us here
They are our memories in our hearts they are there
There is no promise what tomorrow may bring
Let's hope for happiness, joy and everything.

Share a smile with a stranger on the street
Sorry to part and hope someday to meet
So let the old year leave it in the past
But keep the fond memories forever they will last.

So what will tomorrow bring we will never know
For every day is the same day happily we will go
Keep your friends close at hand and keep them ever so dear
They will always be with you close and near.

Charles F. Meek

My Dear Old Grannie

I was visiting my old Grannie at her wee but and ben
Down by the loch side we visited her now and then
We looked over the loch to the mountains far above
Fields of purple heather our Grannie full of love.

Listen and you will hear the skirl O' the pipes in the glen below
People going by, to the piper to say hello
The old castle still stands where battles were once fought
The Lion Rampant flying high and quite taut.

The Monarch of the Glen stands proudly and head held high
As he bellows to his mate as she trots on by
I like being at the but and ben, my Grannie's heilan hame
She is the love of my life, I'm proud to carry her name.

So a welcome to you all, friends, kith and kin
C'mon in sit ye down, and meet the dear auld yin
She will give you a wee drink, and a sprig O' white heather
And thank you kindly for your time and the wee blether
In my dear old Grannie's Heilan Hame.

A Soldier's Valour

'Twas the night before Christmas, I walk on down the street
Hoping to see someone, someone I can meet
You see I have no home, a home to call my own
A bench in the park, that is my home.

I pass the church with lights full ablaze
I hear the singing from inside, so full of grace
I look inside the door, but afraid to go on in
When a hand touches my shoulder,
a voice says, there is warmth within.

I thank this stranger who welcomes me inside,
and sits beside me on a pew
He looks at me as if he knew
We listen to the choir, as they sing Silent Night
I stand and sing along, I sing with all my might.

My voice is cracked with the drinking over the years
The stranger sings with me, he eases all my fears
I tell him I was a soldier and fought in a war long forgot
I was put aside by others, they didn't care, they cared nought.

The old soldier fell asleep in that church pew a Bible for a pillow
An Angel called and said to him, "Soldier come follow
You have served your time, now come rest
In our heavenly eyes, yes, you are one of the best
Your country forgot you and laid you aside
Here in my heavenly home, this is where you will abide."

Charles F. Meek

A Soldier He Was

They tell me you were a soldier of long, long ago
A grandfather I never did get to know
My dad did tell me, that he was a soldier's son
That you went to war, to put the enemy on the run.

The years you fought in were the Fourteen to Eighteen war
I can't imagine the tragedies, the tragedies that you saw
You fought a valiant battle, on the beaches of France you fell
You will always be remembered this I can tell.

Your name is carved in stone on the cenotaph in your hometown
We look at it and pray as we do bow down
I am honoured to be your grandson of a grandfather I never knew
I will remember you on the 11th, as I sit in the church pew
I wear my poppy red, I wear it with pride
I will honour your name, in remembrance I will abide.

Dedicated to My Father's Father
My Grandfather

A Piper of Renown, Keith Easdale

There is a young man who is dear to Eleanor and I
He has a smile and a glint in his eye
He lives in a far off land, but we do often talk and pass the time of day
He is our Keith we're happy he came our way.

He calls us Mum and Pop he makes us so proud
He is our boy, of that there is no doubt
He plays his pipes that can make your hair stand on end
He is so special to us he is not just a friend.

A long time ago he played with the famous SFO
Dancing in the Isles as he played he had you on the go
From the Dark Island to Highland Cathedral
When he played he gave his all.

Yes we are proud of this fine young man
He will go out of his way and help you all he can
Yes he is our Keith he will never let you down
A Piper he is, a Piper of Renown.

Charles F. Meek

A Grandson's Question

Granddad why do those people have a flower on this day?
That is a poppy, son, we wear it on Remembrance Day
But why do you wear it the small child asked
To remember our veterans of their weary task.

Many of my friends fell in wars that have past
The poppy is a symbol that forever will last
Granddad did you fight in those wars gone by
Yes I did he said with a tear in his eye.

Freedom was a hefty price to pay
In Flanders Fields many friends they do lay
Flanders Fields granddad do I need to know
Yes my son that's where the poppies do grow.

Each year at this time we march down the street
Where old friends march and where we meet
We lay our poppies on the cenotaph there
And remember the burdens we did have to bare.

We fought for freedom that was our goal
In life and in death many did fall
So wear your poppy and wear it with pride
Never forget to the fallen we will abide.
We Will Never Forget.

A Christmas Blessing

Christmas day is here, we're in a happy mood
Santa came and left presents and they were all good
We shared the day with friends online
Many of these friends, are yours and also mine.

I spent this day with the love of my life
Of course my loving Eleanor, my ever loving wife
We had young David here for this Christmas day
We missed young Ken, darn he couldn't get away.

This old year will soon be gone a new beginning is in sight
Let us pray for a peaceful year a prayer every night
Let us remember those who have gone keep them in our memories
A toast to absent friends a toast if you please.

Wherever your path leads you let it be straight and true
Hold your head up high let all know that it is you
From Eleanor and I we wish you all a Happy New Year
Let's all go forward without any fear.

Charles F. Meek

A Baby Is Born

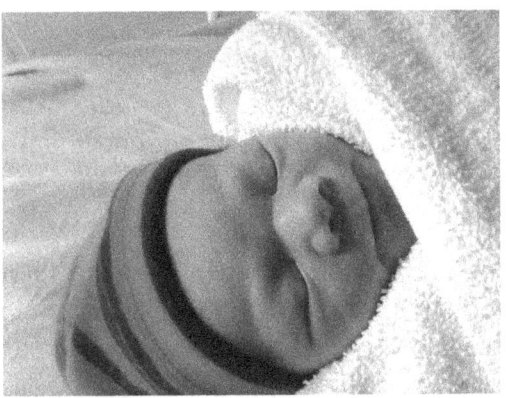

Happiness has come today to two friends of ours
A baby has been born among the roses, a beautiful flower
To John and Beth a grandson to enjoy
Oh they are so happy to have this wee boy.

We know they will care for him in every way they can
Watch him grow and see him become a man
Beth can babysit and look after this wee boy
And John a proud grandad will buy the odd toy.

We are so happy for Mum and Dad too
Treasure this wee boy he is there for both of you
Today is a day of happiness a day filled with joy
Hold him in your arms and love him, he is your loving boy.

Beth and John I see the smile on your faces
Axel is here his face full of Graces.

Some Additional Poems

I hope you have enjoyed the poems and writings in the book. As you have read, I often officiate at funerals and memorial services for our veterans, and members of my branch at the Royal Canadian Legion, as well as for Remembrance Day services.

There are some poems I read at those services, even though I did not write them myself. The words of these poems accent the service. I have listed some of these poems below and provided a link so you may read them and enjoy their meanings.

When Tomorrow Starts Without Me
http://www.poeticexpressions.co.uk/POEMS/Iftomorrowstartswithoutme.htm

Letter from Heaven
http://unforgettableangels.angelstouch16.com/Letter/letter.htm

My First Christmas in Heaven
http://www.utahshare.org/newsletter/2012/11/01/1051/

The Old Comrade
http://www.rcl462.ca/old-comrade.html

Why Wear A Poppy
http://www.veterans.gc.ca/eng/feature/vetweek/comm_guide/poems

Merry Christmas, My Friend
http://www.hymnsandcarolsofchristmas.com/Poetry/merry_christmas_my_friend.htm

Just A Common Soldier
http://vaincourt.homestead.com/common_soldier.html

Sincerely yours,
Charlie

About the Author

Charles F. Meek has lived in Terrace, British Columbia ever since emigrating from Scotland in 1979. He is very involved in his community. Over the years he has been Commanding Officer of 747 Squadron of the local Air Cadets and past President of Royal Canadian Legion Branch 13.

Working for the veterans was first and foremost, and he still hosts the Remembrance Day services from the Tillicum Twin Theatres on November 11th of each year, which is broadcast on CityWest's Community Channel 10. He has also hosted a Scottish radio show, *A Touch O' White Heather*, and television program, *Down in the Glen*. At one time Charlie was a Marriage Commissioner. He enjoyed seeing many happy people and has many fond memories.

Assisting others is a part of his life, and he continues helping people by serving at funeral and memorial services. Now semi-retired, Charlie enjoys fishing on the ocean with friends. Charlie is married to his wife Eleanor, who has inspired many of his poems and writings.

www.ingramcontent.com/pod-product-compliance
Lightning Source LLC
Chambersburg PA
CBHW031659040426
42453CB00006B/347